BANANAS
Cookbook

Printed in the USA by G&R Publishing Co., Waverly, IA

Published and distributed by:

507 Industrial Street
Waverly, IA 50677

ISBN-13: 978-1-56383-152-2
ISBN-10: 1-56383-152-X
Item #3711

Appetizers & Beverages

Mocha Madness Smoothie

2 T. Espresso, ground
2 T. chocolate syrup
1 C. milk

2 bananas
½ C. vanilla frozen yogurt

Mix together in blender and serve.

Fruit Dip

1 C. (8 oz.) plain yogurt
½ medium ripe banana

4 tsp. honey
½ tsp. ground cinnamon

In a blender, combine ingredients; cover and process until smooth. Serve with fresh fruit.

Banana Scotch Muffins

2 bananas, extra ripe
1 egg, beaten
½ C. sugar
¼ C. milk
¼ C. vegetable oil
1 tsp. vanilla extract
1 C. flour

1 C. quick oatmeal
1 tsp. baking powder
½ tsp. baking soda
½ tsp. salt
½ C. chopped nuts, optional
½ C. butterscotch chips

Mix bananas, egg, milk, vanilla and oil; add to dry ingredients. Add nuts and butterscotch chips last. Bake at 400° for 12 to 15 minutes.

Banana Doughnuts

3 C. solid shortening	½ tsp. cinnamon
4 C. flour	½ tsp. nutmeg
¾ C. sugar	¼ C. butter
4 tsp. baking powder	1 C. ripe bananas, mashed
1 tsp. salt	2 eggs, well beaten

In deep fryer, heat shortening to 375°. Mix flour, sugar, baking powder, salt, cinnamon and nutmeg in a large bowl. Cut in butter. Make a well in the center and add the bananas and eggs; mix well. Mix by hand because the dough will be heavy. Turn out on a lightly floured board and roll ½″ thick. Cut with 2½″ doughnut cutter. Deep fry until golden brown. Drain on absorbent paper.

TOPPING:
¾ C. sugar   2 tsp. cinnamon

Combine topping ingredients and dip warm doughnuts in the mixture.

Banana-Oatmeal Muffins

1 C. oatmeal, uncooked
1 C. flour
1 T. baking powder
½ tsp. cinnamon
½ C. skim milk

½ C. mashed bananas
½ C. raisins
¼ C. corn oil
¼ C. packed brown sugar
1 egg white

Combine oatmeal, flour, baking powder and cinnamon. Add remaining ingredients and mix until dry ingredients are moistened. Fill lined muffin cups three-fourths full. Bake at 400° for 20 to 25 minutes.

Can freeze and reheat frozen muffins in microwave on high about 45 seconds per muffin.

Banana Nut Muffins

2 C. flour
¼ C. sugar
1 T. baking powder
½ tsp. salt
1 C. milk

1 egg, beaten
⅓ C. vegetable oil
¾ C. mashed banana
½ C. chopped walnuts

Preheat oven to 400°. Grease a 12-cup muffin pan. Sift flour, sugar, baking powder and salt into a medium bowl; make a depression in the middle. Mix milk, egg, oil, banana and walnuts in a small bowl. Pour mixture into the depression. Mix batter just until moistened; do not over mix. Spoon batter into muffin cups. Bake until muffins are golden brown, about 15 minutes.

Banana Split Smoothies

2 ripe bananas
1-8 oz. can crushed pineapple,
   drained
1½ C. milk
½ C. sliced strawberries

2 T. honey
5 ice cubes
Whipped topping
Chocolate syrup
Maraschino cherries

In a blender, combine bananas, milk, strawberries and honey. Gradually add ice; blending until slushy. Pour into chilled glasses. Garnish with whipped topping, chocolate syrup and cherries.

Banana Coconut Loaf

2 eggs	½ C. flaked coconut
1 C. white sugar	1½ tsp. baking powder
½ C. butter, melted	½ tsp. baking soda
1 C. mashed bananas	½ tsp. salt
½ tsp. almond extract	½ C. chopped walnuts
1½ C. all-purpose flour	½ C. maraschino cherries, chopped

Mix together flour, coconut, baking powder, baking soda, salt, chopped walnuts and cherries. Break eggs in a mixing bowl; beat until light and frothy. Add sugar and melted butter or margarine; beat well. Stir in mashed banana and flavoring. Add flour mixture; stir just to combine. Spoon into greased 9 x 5 x 3″ loaf pan. Bake at 350° for 1 hour, or until toothpick inserted in center comes out clean. Let stand 10 minutes. Remove from pan; cool.

Fruit Smoothies

1 medium firm banana
1 C. orange juice
1 C. fat-free plain yogurt

1 C. frozen strawberries or
   raspberries
6 pkts. artificial sweetener

Peel and cut banana into chunks. Place in a plastic freezer bag. Seal and freeze overnight. Place all ingredients in blender. Cover and process until smooth.

Apricot Banana Bread

⅓ C. butter or margarine,
   softened
⅔ C. sugar
2 eggs
1 C. mashed ripe bananas
   (2 to 3 medium)
¼ C. buttermilk
1¼ C. all-purpose flour

1 tsp. baking powder
½ tsp. soda
½ tsp. salt
1 C. 100% bran cereal
¾ C. chopped dried apricots
   (about 6 oz.)
½ c. walnuts

In a mixing bowl, cream butter and sugar. Add eggs; mix well. Combine bananas and buttermilk. Combine the flour, baking powder, baking soda and salt. Add to creamed mixture alternately with banana mixture. Stir in bran, apricots and nuts. Pour into greased 9 x 5 x 3″ loaf pan. Bake at 350° for 55 to 60 minutes or until bread tests done. Cool 10 minutes before removing from pan to a wire rack.

Double Chocolate Banana Muffins

1½ C. all-purpose flour
1 C. sugar
½ C. baking cocoa
1 tsp. baking soda
½ tsp. salt
¼ tsp. baking powder

1½ C. mashed ripe bananas
⅓ C. vegetable oil
1 egg
1 C. (6 oz.) miniature semi-sweet
   chocolate chips

In a large bowl, combine the first six ingredients. In a small bowl, combine bananas, oil and egg; stir into dry ingredients just until moistened. Fold in chocolate chips. Fill greased or paper lined muffin cups three-fourths full. Bake at 350° for 20 to 25 minutes or until muffins test done.

Pineapple Slush

1-5¼ oz. can pineapple tidbits,
   drained
1 medium banana, chilled

¼ C. milk
2 C. pineapple sherbet

Combine all ingredients in blender; process until smooth.

Fruit Slush

1-6 oz. can frozen lemonade
1-6 oz. can frozen orange juice
2 boxes frozen strawberries
1-20 oz. can crushed pineapple,
   undrained

1 C. sugar
1 small bottle maraschino cherries,
   cut up and undrained
3 to 4 bananas, quarter, then slice
1 C. water

Mix and freeze. About 2 hours before serving, take from freezer. Stir with fork as it breaks ups. Serve slightly frozen.

Banana Punch

4 C. sugar
6 C. water
5 bananas, mashed

2-12 oz. cans frozen orange juice
1-12 oz. can frozen lemonade
1-48 oz. can pineapple juice

Heat sugar and water. Cool, then add bananas and juices; freeze. When serving, add equal amounts of 7-Up.

Banana-Wheat Germ Muffins

1½ C. flour
1 C. wheat germ, toasted
½ C. brown sugar
1 T. baking powder
½ tsp. salt
1 tsp. ground nutmeg

½ C. egg substitute
½ C. skim milk
¼ C. polyunsaturated oil
  (canola oil)
1 C. mashed bananas
½ C. walnuts

Heat oven to 425°. Spray muffin tin with no-stick spray. In mixing bowl, stir all dry ingredients except nuts. Beat other ingredients in a separate bowl until smooth. Add dry ingredients; blend until well moistened. Stir in nuts. Spoon batter into muffin cups and bake for 20 minutes until rich brown and serve warm.

Banana Poppy Seed Bread

1 C. sugar
½ C. margarine
2 eggs
2 C. all-purpose flour

1 tsp. baking soda
3 bananas, mashed
1 tsp. vanilla
¼ C. poppy seeds

Cream sugar and margarine; add eggs and beat. Add flour and soda; beat until blended. Next, add bananas, vanilla and poppy seeds. Beat until mixed well. Bake in two 3½ x 7″ greased loaf pans, for about 45 to 50 minutes at 350°.

Chocolate Chunk Banana Bread

2 eggs, lightly beaten
1 C. mashed ripe bananas
⅓ C. vegetable oil
¼ C. milk
2 C. all-purpose flour
1 C. sugar

2 tsp. baking powder
¼ tsp. salt
1-4 oz. pkg. sweet chocolate
　squares, coarsely chopped
½ C. chopped nuts

Heat oven to 350°. Stir eggs, bananas, oil and milk until well blended. Add flour, sugar, baking powder and salt; stir until just moistened. Stir in chocolate and nuts. Pour into greased 9 x 5″ loaf pan. Bake for 55 minutes or until toothpick inserted in center comes out clean. Cool in pan 10 minutes. Remove from pan to cool on wire rack.

Banana Slush Punch

4 ripe bananas
2 C. white sugar
3 C. water
1-46 oz. can pineapple juice

2-12 oz. cans frozen orange juice
   concentrate
1-12 oz. can frozen lemonade
   concentrate
3 C. water
3 liters ginger ale

In a blender, combine bananas, sugar and 3 cups water; blend until smooth. Pour into a large bowl and stir in pineapple juice. Blend in orange juice concentrate, lemonade concentrate and 3 cups water. Divide into 3 plastic containers and freeze until solid. Remove from freezer 3 to 4 hours before serving. Using one portion at a time, place slush in a punch bowl and pour in 1 liter of ginger ale for each.

Banana-Blueberry Muffins

2 extra-ripe bananas
2 eggs
1 C. firmly packed brown sugar
½ C. margarine
1 C. blueberries

1 tsp. vanilla
2¼ C. flour
2 tsp. baking powder
½ tsp. ground cinnamon
½ tsp. salt

Purée bananas in blender. In medium bowl, combine 1 cup puréed bananas, eggs, sugar and margarine until blended. Stir in blueberries and vanilla. In large bowl, combine flour, baking powder, cinnamon and salt. Stir banana mixture into flour mixture until evenly moistened. Spoon batter into well greased 2½″ muffin cups. Bake in 350° oven 25 to 30 minutes or until center comes out clean. Serve warm.

Creamsicle Smoothie

1 C. strawberries
1 C. fresh orange juice

2 bananas
1 C. vanilla frozen yogurt

Place in a blender; mix well and serve.

Banana Bread

1 C. sugar
1 C. brown sugar, packed
¾ C. margarine
1 C. milk
2 eggs
3 bananas, very ripe, mashed
1 T. grated orange rind

2 tsp. baking powder
1 tsp. soda
½ tsp. salt
3 C. flour
1 tsp. vanilla
1 C. pecans, chopped

Cream sugars and margarine. Add other ingredients in order given; beat 3 minutes. Pour batter into two greased and floured loaf pans. Bake at 350° for about 1 hour or until toothpick inserted in the center comes out clean.

Banana-Blueberry Bread

1 C. sugar
½ C. oil
1 C. mashed bananas
½ C. blueberry yogurt
1 tsp. vanilla

2 eggs
2 C. flour
1 tsp. baking soda
½ tsp. salt
1 C. frozen blueberries

Grease and flour a large loaf pan. Beat sugar and oil. Add bananas, yogurt, vanilla and eggs; mix well. Add flour, baking soda and salt until blended. Stir in blueberries. Bake at 350° for 45 to 50 minutes.

Banana Bran Muffins

½ C. butter or margarine, softened
1 C. sugar
2 eggs
3 medium ripe bananas, mashed
½ C. buttermilk

1½ C. flour
1½ tsp. baking soda
½ tsp. salt
1 C. Raisin Bran
1 C. miniature semi-sweet
   chocolate chips
½ C. chopped pecans

In a mixing bowl, cream butter and sugar. Add the eggs, bananas and buttermilk. Combine the flour, baking soda and salt; stir into creamed mixture just until moistened. Fold in the cereal, chocolate chips and pecans. Fill greased or paper lined muffin cups two-thirds full. Bake at 350° for 23 to 25 minutes or until a toothpick comes out clean. Cool for 5 minutes before removing from pan.

Fruity Yogurt Muffins

1¾ C. all-purpose flour
⅓ C. granulated sugar
2 tsp. baking powder
½ tsp. ground cinnamon
¼ tsp. salt
1 egg, beaten

⅔ C. mashed bananas
    (about 2 bananas)
½ C. strawberry low-fat yogurt*
¼ C. cooking oil
2 T. brown sugar

Grease twelve 2½″ muffin cups; set aside. In a medium mixing bowl, combine flour, granulated sugar, baking powder, cinnamon and salt. In another medium mixing bowl, stir together egg, mashed bananas, yogurt and oil. Add banana-yogurt mixture, all at once, to the flour mixture; stir just until moistened. Batter will be a little lumpy. Fill muffin cups three-fourths full. Sprinkle with brown sugar. Bake in 400° oven for 20 to 25 minutes or until golden brown. Cool in muffin pan on a wire rack for 5 minutes. Remove from muffin pans and serve warm.

*Can substitute your favorite fruit flavored yogurt.

Banana Crescents

¼ C. chopped salted peanuts
¼ C. flaked coconut
¼ C. confectioners' sugar
¼ tsp. cinnamon
¼ tsp. nutmeg

1 can Pillsbury refrigerated crescent
  dinner rolls
2 bananas, cut in half crosswise
1 T. lemon juice
¼ C. maple syrup
¼ C. sifted confectioners' sugar

Combine peanuts, coconut, ¼ cup confectioners' sugar, cinnamon and nutmeg. Unroll crescent dough and separate into 4 rectangles. Place rectangles of dough on ungreased cookie sheet. Sprinkle peanut mixture over each dough rectangle. Dip each banana half in lemon juice, then in maple syrup. Place each banana half on narrow end of dough rectangle and roll up, ending with seam side down. Pinch edges well to seal. Bake at 400° for 12 to 15 minutes or until golden brown. Sprinkle with ¼ cup confectioners' sugar while warm. Cut each roll into two or four pastries.

Salads & Veggies

Banana Fluff

1-3 oz. pkg. raspberry
   or strawberry gelatin
Dash of salt
1 C. boiling water

1 can crushed pineapple
1 C. mashed bananas
1 C. finely cut marshmallows

Dissolve jello and salt in boiling water. Drain pineapple, reserving juice. Add enough water to pineapple juice to make ¾ cup. Add to gelatin; chill until very thick. Beat with mixer until fluffy. Fold in drained pineapple, bananas and marshmallows. Put in mold; chill.

Banana Lettuce Toss

⅓ C. half and half
⅓ C. salad dressing
2 T. sugar

½ head lettuce, chopped
2 bananas, sliced
¼ C. cashews

Mix together first three ingredients. Pour dressing over lettuce, bananas and cashews; toss lightly. Can easily be doubled.

Dr. Pepper Fruit Mold

1-3 oz. pkg. raspberry gelatin
1¼ C. Dr. Pepper beverage,
    boiling
1-10 oz. pkg. frozen raspberries

¾ C. canned crushed pineapple,
    drained
1 large banana, sliced
¼ C. chopped pecans

Dissolve gelatin in boiling Dr. Pepper. Add partially thawed raspberries. Stir until berries are separated. Chill until mixture is thickened. Fold in remaining ingredients. Pour into mold. Chill until firm; unmold. Serve with Sour Cream Fruit Dressing.

SOUR CREAM FRUIT DRESSING: Combine 1 cup sour cream with 1½ cups miniature marshmallows, 1 tablespoon sugar and 2½ tablespoons lemon juice. Chill several hours. Stir well before serving.

Banana Whip

6 medium bananas
1 T. lemon juice
½ tsp. vanilla
4 egg whites, whipped

6 T. confectioners' sugar
½ C. nuts, chopped
⅛ tsp. salt

Mash the bananas through a ricer or food mill. Beat in the sugar, lemon juice, vanilla and nuts. Whip the egg whites with the salt until stiff. Fold them into banana mixture. Place in baking dish and bake at 325° for about 30 minutes. Serve hot or cold.

Melon Salad

3 oranges
3 cans pineapple, drained
3 bananas

1 cantaloupe, cubed or in balls
Watermelon, cubed or in balls

DRESSING:
2 T. cornstarch
¾ C. sugar
½ C. water

Juice and rind of 1 orange
Juice from ½ lemon

Cook first three dressing ingredients until thick. Add juice and rind from orange and lemon; chill. Chill prepared fruit. Add bananas to dressing and combine with chilled fruit at serving time. Serve in empty watermelon shell.

Frozen Cranberry Banana Salad

1-20 oz. can pineapple tidbits
5 medium firm bananas, halved
   lengthwise and sliced
1-16 oz. can whole-berry
   cranberry sauce

½ C. sugar
1-12 oz. carton frozen whipped
   topping, thawed
½ C. chopped walnuts

Drain pineapple juice into a medium bowl; set pineapple aside. Add bananas to the juice. In a large bowl, combine cranberry sauce and sugar. Remove bananas, discarding juice and add to cranberry mixture. Stir in pineapple, whipped topping and nuts. Pour into a 13 x 9 x 2″ dish. Freeze until solid. Remove from the freezer 15 minutes before cutting.

Fruited Pistachio Pudding

1-3.4 oz. instant pistachio flavored
   pudding mix
1-8 oz. carton frozen whipped topping,
   thawed
2 T. salad dressing or mayonnaise

1-16 oz. can fruit cocktail, undrained
1-8 oz. can crushed pineapple,
   undrained
2 bananas, sliced
1 C. miniature marshmallows

In a large bowl, combine pudding mix, whipped topping and salad dressing; mix well.
Fold in remaining ingredients. Leave in bowl or spoon into individual serving dishes.
Serve immediately or chill.

Strawberry Whip Salad

1-10 oz. container frozen strawberries
3 bananas, sliced
2 C. small curd cottage cheese
¾ C. miniature marshmallows

1-3 oz. box strawberry gelatin
1-12 oz. container whipped topping
Grated nuts, optional

Thaw berries in a large bowl. Add bananas and cottage cheese. Pour dry jello over mixture. Stir, then add marshmallows, Cool Whip and grated nuts, if desired.

Frozen Fruit Cups

2-10 oz. frozen strawberries
1-12 oz. frozen orange juice
2-20 oz. crushed pineapple

1-16 oz. mandarin oranges
⅓ C. lemon juice
4 pkgs. artificial sweetener
6 bananas, sliced

Soak bananas in lemon juice. Mix all ingredients. Put in ½-cup individual serving cups. Take from freezer 1 hour before serving.

Seven Fruit Salad

½ C. lime juice
½ C. water
½ C. sugar
2 medium nectarines, thinly sliced
1 large firm banana, thinly sliced

1 pt. blueberries
1 pt. strawberries, sliced
1½ C. watermelon balls
1 C. grapes
1 kiwi fruit, peeled and chopped

In a bowl, combine lime juice, water and sugar; stir until sugar is dissolved. Add nectarines and bananas, toss to coat. In a 2½-quart glass bowl, combine the remaining fruits. Add nectarine mixture; stir gently. Cover and refrigerate for 1 hour. Serve with slotted spoon.

Duchess Salad

1 C. macaroni
2 apples, diced
2 bananas, diced
1 C. crushed pineapple, drained

1 C. mini-marshmallows
½ C. dates
1 C. whipped cream
½ C. salad dressing

Cook, drain, rinse and chill macaroni. Add fruit and marshmallows. Mix whipped cream and salad dressing together. Stir all together and chill.

Frozen Fruit Salad

1 C. water
1 C. sugar
2 cartons frozen strawberries, thawed

1-20 oz. can crushed pineapple
1-20 oz. can apricot halves, drained
4 to 5 bananas, sliced

Mix sugar and water. Bring to a boil; cool. Mix all ingredients together with the sugar syrup. Spoon into small paper cups and freeze. Peel off the paper cups to serve on lettuce as a salad.

Fruit Soup

3 T. Minute Tapioca
1 C. peach juice
⅓ C. sugar
Dash of salt
1 C. water

1 can mandarin oranges, drained
2 C. peaches
1-6 oz. can frozen orange juice
1-16 oz. pkg. frozen strawberries
2 bananas

Boil tapioca, peach juice, sugar and salt for 6 minutes; stirring constantly. Remove from heat and add 1 cup water, mandarin oranges, peaches, orange juice, strawberries and bananas; mix well and refrigerate.

Fresh fruit in season can be added. Also good served with lime sherbet.

Banana Split Salad

1-8 oz. can crushed pineapple
2 C. water
1-3 oz. pkg. lemon gelatin
8 large marshmallows
2 bananas, sliced
2 tsp. lemon juice
¼ C. sugar

5 tsp. all-purpose flour
Dash of salt
1 egg, beaten
1 T. butter or margarine
1 C. heavy cream, whipped
¼ C. chopped pecans

Drain pineapple, saving ½ cup juice and set aside. In saucepan, bring water to boil. Remove from heat; add gelatin and marshmallows. Stir until dissolved; chill until partially set. Toss bananas with lemon juice. Fold bananas and pineapple into gelatin. Pour into 8″ square dish; chill until firm. Combine the sugar, flour and salt in saucepan. Stir in egg and saved pineapple juice. Cook and stir over low heat until thickened. Remove from heat. Stir in butter and cool. Stir in whipped cream. Spread over gelatin, sprinkle with pecans. Chill overnight.

Creamy Banana-Rice Pudding

1 egg
½ C. milk
2 C. cooked rice (warm or cold)

1 ripe banana, mashed
½ tsp. (large pkg.) artificial sweetener
¼ tsp. nutmeg or cinnamon

Whisk egg in milk in large microwavable bowl. Microwave on high for 2 minutes. (Egg will be slightly cooked.) Stir in rice, mashed banana and sweetener. Top with nutmeg. Eat warm or cold.

Mountain Dew Salad

2 pkgs. lemon gelatin
2 C. very hot water
2 or 3 bananas
2 C. mini-marshmallows

2 C. Mountain Dew
1 C. crushed pineapple
1-8 oz. carton whipped topping
1 pkg. lemon instant pudding

Mix gelatin with hot water. Add pop, bananas, marshmallows and pineapple. Let sit in refrigerator. Mix instant pudding as on package. Fold whipped topping into pudding. Spread on top of gelatin mix; refrigerate.

Layered Strawberry Salad

2 pkgs. strawberry gelatin
2 C. boiling water
2 pkgs. frozen strawberries

2 mashed bananas
1-#2 can crushed pineapple, drained
1 carton sour cream

Mix gelatin with water. Add partly thawed strawberries, pineapple and bananas. Place half of mixture in bottom of 9 x 12″ pan. Place in refrigerator and let set. Don't let it get too solid so that the sour cream will stick. Remove from refrigerator and spread sour cream over bottom layer Add remaining gelatin mixture and put back in refrigerator.

Grandmother's Orange Salad

1-11 oz. can mandarin oranges
1-8 oz. can crushed pineapple
Water

1-6 oz. pkg. orange flavored gelatin
1 pt. orange sherbet, sliced
2 bananas, sliced

Drain oranges and pineapple, reserving juices. Set oranges and pineapple aside. Add water to juices to measure 2 cups. Place in a saucepan and bring to a boil. Pour over gelatin in a large bowl. Stir in sherbet until smooth. Chill until partially set (watch carefully). Fold in oranges, pineapple and bananas. Pour into an oiled 6-cup mold. Chill until firm.

Four Fruit Salad

1-20 oz. can pineapple chunks
½ C. sugar
2 T. cornstarch
1 T. lemon juice
⅓ C. orange juice

1-11 oz. can mandarin oranges,
   drained
3 to 4 unpeeled apples, chopped
2 to 3 bananas, sliced

Drain pineapple, reserving ¾ cup juice. In a saucepan, combine sugar and cornstarch. Add pineapple juice, orange juice and lemon juice. Cook and stir over medium heat until thickened and bubbly; cook and stir 1 minute longer. Remove from the heat; set aside. In a bowl, combine pineapple chunks, oranges, apples and bananas. Pour warm sauce over the fruit; stir gently to coat. Cover and refrigerate.

Snicker Salad

1 C. milk
1-3 oz. pkg. instant vanilla pudding
8 oz. whipped topping

1 to 2 Snickers
2 Granny Smith apples
1 to 2 bananas

Combine milk and instant pudding. When set, stir in whipped topping. Cut up apples, Snickers and sliced bananas. Add to mixture shortly before serving, so that fruit stays fresh and Snickers don't melt.

Fruit Medley Salad

½ C. salad dressing
¼ C. sour cream
1-11 oz. can mandarin orange
    segments, drained
2 bananas, sliced

1-8 oz. can pineapple chunks in
    juice, drained
1 C. miniature marshmallows
1 C. coconut

Mix dressing and sour cream in large bowl. Add fruit, marshmallows and coconut; mix lightly. Refrigerate several hours or overnight.

Frozen Salad

1-8 oz. pkg. cream cheese
1 T. lemon juice
½ C. salad dressing
½ C. sugar
1 C. heavy cream, whipped

1 can fruit cocktail, drained
1 can pineapple, drained
2 to 3 bananas
1 pkg. fresh or frozen strawberries

Soften cream cheese; add lemon juice and salad dressing. Whip cream; add sugar. Combine whipped cream mixture with the cream cheese mixture. Add drained fruit cocktail, pineapple, diced bananas and strawberries. Mix well and freeze in 9 x 9″ pan.

Main Dishes

Apple-Banana Oatmeal

1 C. water
1 T. orange juice concentrate
½ C. chopped unpeeled tart apple
¼ C. sliced firm banana
¼ C. raisins

¼ tsp. salt
⅛ tsp. ground cinnamon
⅔ C. quick cooking oatmeal
¼ to ⅓ C. oat bran
Brown sugar, optional

In a saucepan, combine water, orange juice concentrate, apple, banana, raisins, salt and cinnamon. Bring to a boil. Stir in oats and oat bran. Cook for 1 to 2 minutes, stirring occasionally. Sprinkle with brown sugar.

Banana Pancakes

1 C. all-purpose flour
1 T. white sugar
2 tsp. baking powder
¼ tsp. salt

1 egg, beaten
1 C. milk
2 T. vegetable oil
2 ripe bananas, mashed

Combine flour, white sugar, baking powder and salt. In another bowl, mix together the egg, milk, vegetable oil and bananas. Stir flour mixture into banana mixture. Heat a lightly oiled griddle over medium-high heat. Pour batter onto griddle, using approximately ¼ cup for each pancake. Cook until pancakes are golden brown on both sides. Serve hot.

Banana Waffles

2¼ C. sifted all-purpose flour
4 tsp. baking powder
1½ T. sugar
¾ tsp. salt

2 eggs, beaten
1¾ C. milk
¾ C. mashed banana (1 banana)
½ C. salad oil

Sift together first four ingredients. Mix together eggs, milk, banana and oil until blended. Add banana mixture to dry ingredients, stirring only until moistened. Pour one-third of the batter onto preheated waffle baker. Bake until brown, about 5 minutes. Repeat with remaining batter.

Wholesome Banana Oat Pancakes

¾ C. rolled oats
⅔ C. whole wheat flour
½ tsp. salt
1 tsp. baking powder
½ tsp. soda
½ tsp. ground nutmeg

1 large egg
¾ C. mashed ripe banana
¾ C. buttermilk
2 T. vegetable oil
½ tsp. vanilla

Combine dry ingredients. Beat banana with egg until well blended. Add buttermilk, oil and vanilla; beat until smooth. Add dry ingredients to banana mixture. Pour on heated griddle, using ¼ cup mix per pancake.

Peanut Butter and
Banana Sandwich

2 slices whole wheat bread   1 banana
½ C. peanut butter

Put 2 slices of whole wheat bread on a paper plate. Next combine the peanut
butter and banana in a bowl; mix well. Spread mixture on bread and serve with
plenty of napkins.

South Seas Chicken and Bananas

¼ C. lemon juice
1-14 oz. can sweetened
  condensed milk
⅓ C. milk
½ C. flaked coconut
⅛ tsp. ground cardamom

6 very firm bananas, halved
  lengthwise
3 C. corn flake crumbs
5 to 6 lbs. chicken pieces
¾ C. butter or margarine,
  melted (divided)
Sliced kiwi fruit and star fruit, optional

In a food processor or blender, blend the lemon juice, condensed milk, milk, coconut and cardamom until smooth. Pour into a bowl. Dip bananas into milk mixture; roll in corn flakes and set aside. Dip chicken into remaining milk mixture; roll in the remaining corn flakes and place in two greased 13 x 9 x 2″ baking pans. Drizzle with ½ cup of the melted butter. Bake, uncovered, at 350° for 1 hour. Arrange bananas over chicken. Drizzle with remaining butter. Bake 15 minutes longer or until chicken juices run clear. Garnish with kiwi and star fruit, if desired.

Hawaiian Pork Roast

1-3 to 4 lb. boneless pork
   shoulder roast, trimmed
4 tsp. liquid smoke

4 tsp. soy sauce
2 ripe bananas, unpeeled
½ C. water

Place the roast on a 22 x 18″ piece of heavy duty foil; sprinkle with liquid smoke and soy sauce. Wash bananas and place at the base of each side of roast. Pull sides of foil up around meat; add water. Seal foil tightly; wrap again with another large piece of foil. Place in a shallow baking pan; refrigerate overnight, turning several times. Place foil wrapped meat in a roasting pan. Bake at 400° for 1 hour. Reduce heat to 325° and continue baking for 3½ hours. Drain; discard bananas and liquid. Shred meat with a fork.

Desserts

Banana Split Cheesecake Squares

2 C. (about 14 whole) graham
   cracker crumbs
⅓ C. margarine, melted
1 C. sugar, divided
3-8 oz. pkgs. cream cheese,
   softened
1 tsp. vanilla

3 eggs
½ C. mashed bananas
1 C. halved strawberries
1 banana, sliced and tossed with
   1 tsp. lemon juice
1-8 oz. can chunked pineapple,
   drained

Mix crushed graham cracker crumbs, margarine and ¼ cup of the sugar. Press onto bottom of 13 x 9˝ baking pan. Mix cream cheese, remaining ¾ cup sugar and vanilla with electric mixer until well blended. Add eggs; mix until blended. Stir in the mashed banana. Pour mixture into crust. Bake at 350° for 30 minutes or until center is almost set; cool. Refrigerate 3 hours or overnight. Top with strawberries, sliced banana and pineapple. If desired, sprinkle with nuts and drizzle with chocolate syrup. Cut into squares.

Pink Champagne Salad

8 oz. cream cheese
¾ C. sugar
2 bananas, mashed

1 can crushed pineapple, drained
1 box frozen strawberries, thawed
8 oz. whipped topping

Mix cream cheese, sugar, bananas, pineapple and strawberries in blender. Transfer into large bowl and fold in whipped topping. Put salad into 9 x 13″ glass dish and freeze. Before serving, set out dish for a few minutes for ease of cutting.

Sour Cream Banana Spice Cake

2 eggs, separated
½ C. (1 stick) butter
1½ C. brown sugar, packed
2 C. flour
1 tsp. soda
1 tsp. cinnamon

½ tsp. salt
½ tsp. ground cloves
½ C. ripe bananas, mashed
½ C. sour cream
1 tsp. vanilla
½ C. finely chopped nuts

Beat egg whites until stiff, but not dry; set aside. Cream together butter and sugar. Beat in egg yolks. Sift flour with soda, salt and spices. Mix together bananas, sour cream and vanilla. Add flour mixture to creamed mixture alternately with banana mixture. Fold in beaten egg whites. Pour into greased 9″ square cake pan. Sprinkle nutmeats over top and if desired, a little cinnamon-sugar. Bake at 350° for about 45 to 50 minutes. Cut into squares and serve warm.

Fruit Pizza

1-17 oz. pkg. sugar cookie dough
1-8 oz. pkg. cream cheese
½ C. powdered sugar
Fruit such as: bananas, grapes,
    strawberries, kiwi, pineapple, etc.

½ C. sugar
½ C. orange juice
2 T. lemon juice
1½ T. cornstarch
6 T. water

Roll cookie dough onto a greased pizza pan. Bake at 350° for 10 minutes. Mix cream cheese and powdered sugar together; spread on cooled cookie dough. Cut up fruit and place on cream cheese mixture. Combine sugar, orange juice, lemon juice, cornstarch and water together. Boil for 1 minute. Cool and pour over fruit. Refrigerate until serving time.

Banana-Chocolate Cake

2¼ C. sifted cake flour
1 tsp. baking powder
¾ tsp. baking soda
1 tsp. salt
⅔ C. shortening
1½ C. sugar

1 tsp. vanilla
2 eggs
2-1 oz. squares unsweetened
    chocolate, melted
1 C. mashed bananas
½ C. buttermilk

Sift together first four ingredients. Cream shortening, sugar and vanilla together until fluffy. Add eggs, one at a time, beating well after each addition. Blend in chocolate. Add dry ingredients alternately with bananas and milk, beating until well blended. Turn into two greased 9″ layer pans and bake at 350° for 30 to 40 minutes. Fill and frost cooled cakes with a butter frosting.

Banana Split Cream Puffs

1 C. water
½ C. butter or margarine
1 C. all-purpose flour
¼ tsp. salt
4 eggs
12 scoops vanilla ice cream

1 C. sliced fresh strawberries
1 large or 2 medium bananas, thinly
  sliced
1-8 oz. can pineapple tidbits, drained
½ C. hot fudge sauce

In a saucepan over medium heat, bring water and butter to a boil. Add flour and salt all at once; stir until a smooth ball forms. Remove from the heat and let stand 5 minutes. Add eggs, one at a time, beating well after each addition. Beat until mixture is smooth and shiny, about 3 minutes. Drop by rounded tablespoonfuls onto a greased baking sheet. Bake at 400° for 30 to 35 minutes or until golden brown. Transfer to a wire rack. Immediately split puffs open; remove tops and set aside. Discard soft dough from inside. Cool puffs. Fill each with a scoop of ice cream and top with fruit. Drizzle with hot fudge sauce. Replace tops and serve immediately.

Chocolate Banana Cream Pie

1-9″ pastry shell or crumb crust
1¼ C. sugar
⅓ C. cocoa
⅓ C. cornstarch
¼ tsp. salt

3 C. milk
3 T. butter or margarine
1½ tsp. vanilla
2 medium bananas, sliced
Whipped topping
Additional banana slices, optional

Bake pastry shell; set aside. Combine sugar, cocoa, cornstarch and salt in medium saucepan; gradually add milk, stirring until smooth. Cook over medium heat, stirring constantly until mixture boils; boil and stir 3 minutes. Remove from heat; blend in butter and vanilla. Pour into bowl; press plastic wrap directly onto surface. Cool to room temperature. Cover bottom of cooled shell with small amount of filling. Arrange banana slices over filling; cover with remaining filling. Chill 3 to 4 hours or until firm. Garnish with whipped topping and banana slices.

Pina Colada Freeze

1 large ripe banana, mashed
1-20 oz. can crushed pineapple,
   drained

⅔ C. salad dressing
⅔ C. cream of coconut
2 C. whipped topping, thawed

Combine banana, pineapple, salad dressing and cream of coconut; mix well. Fold in whipped toppiong. Spoon mixture into 9 x 5″ loaf pan; cover. Freeze until firm. Remove from freezer and place in refrigerator for 30 minutes before serving. Sprinkle with toasted flaked coconut, if desired. Garnish with fresh fruit.

Fruit and Cereal Brunch Cake

1 C. Total cereal
1 C. orange juice
1 egg
¼ C. oil
2 small bananas, sliced
1½ C. flour
¾ C. sugar
1 tsp. baking soda
¾ tsp. cinnamon
½ tsp. salt

STREUSEL TOPPING:
½ C. brown sugar
¼ C. flour
½ tsp. cinnamon
¼ C. margarine, softened
½ C. chopped nuts

Mix orange juice and cereal together; let set for a few minutes. Add egg, oil and bananas; mix well. Add flour, sugar, soda, cinnamon and salt. Stir until well mixed. Pour in a greased 8 x 8″ pan. Bake for 40 minutes at 350°. Remove from oven and cover with Streusel Topping. Put under broiler for a few minutes to brown topping. Watch closely!

Creamy Banana Pudding

1-14 oz. sweetened
  condensed milk
1½ C. cold water
1-3½ oz. pkg. instant vanilla
  pudding

2 C. whipped topping
36 vanilla wafers
3 medium bananas, sliced and
  dipped in lemon juice

In large mixing bowl, combine sweetened condensed milk and water. Add pudding mix; beat until well blended. Chill 5 minutes. Fold in whipped topping. Spoon 1 cup pudding mixture into 2½-quart round glass serving bowl. Top with one-third each of the vanilla wafers, bananas and pudding. Repeat layering twice, ending with pudding mixture; chill thoroughly. Garnish as desired. Refrigerate leftovers.

TIP: Mixture can be layered in individual serving dishes.

Chocolate-Covered Banana Pops

3 firm, large bananas
9 wooden popsicle sticks
2 C. semi-sweet chocolate chips
  or milk chocolate chips

2 T. vegetable shortening
1½ C. chopped almonds

Cut each banana into thirds. Insert wooden stick into each banana piece; place on tray covered with waxed paper. Freeze until firm (about 1 hour). In top of a double boiler over hot, not boiling water, melt chocolate chips and shortening. Remove bananas from freezer just before dipping. Dip each banana into warm chocolate. Allow excess to drip off. Immediately roll in almonds. Cover; return to freezer. Serve frozen.

Banana Custard Pudding

½ C. sugar
1 T. cornstarch
⅛ tsp. salt
1½ C. milk

3 egg yolks, beaten
1 tsp. vanilla
1 medium firm banana, sliced

In a saucepan, combine sugar, cornstarch and salt. Gradually add milk; cook and stir over medium heat until mixture comes to a boil. Cook and stir 2 minutes longer. Stir a small amount into the egg yolks; return all to pan. Cook and stir until thickened. Remove from heat; stir in vanilla. Chill for 1 hour. Just before serving, fold in banana.

Orangey Baked Bananas

¼ C. orange juice
1 T. granulated sugar
2 tsp. packed brown sugar
¼ tsp. ground cinnamon

¼ tsp. ground nutmeg
Dash of ground cloves
1 tsp. grated orange peel
3 large, firm bananas, peeled

In microwave safe 1-cup glass measuring cup, combine orange juice, sugars, cinnamon, nutmeg, cloves and orange peel. Stir until sugars dissolve. Microwave on high for 45 seconds. Cut bananas in half lengthwise, then in thirds crosswise. Arrange banana pieces in a 9″ microwave safe pie plate. Pour sauce over bananas. Microwave on high for 2 minutes. Rearrange, moving outside pieces to center of dish. Baste; microwave on high for 1 to 2 minutes. Serve warm.

Banana Carrot Cake

1¼ C. oil
4 large eggs
1½ tsp. baking soda
3 C. sifted flour
1 C. nuts, chopped

2 C. sugar
2 tsp. baking powder
2 C. grated carrots
2 C. mashed bananas

Mix ingredients; blend well. Pour into two well greased loaf pans. Bake in preheated 350° oven until center springs back. This freezes well.

Banana-Sour Cream Bars

1½ C. white sugar
1 C. dairy sour cream
½ C. margarine or butter, softened
2 eggs
1½ C. mashed bananas
    (about 3 large)
2 tsp. vanilla
2 C. all-purpose flour
¼ tsp. salt

1 tsp. baking soda
½ C. chopped nuts
FROSTING:
2 C. powdered sugar
¼ C. margarine or butter,
    softened
1½ tsp. vanilla
2 T. hot water

Heat oven to 375°. Mix sugar, sour cream, margarine and eggs in large mixing bowl on low speed for 1 minute, scraping bowl occasionally. Beat in bananas and vanilla on low speed 30 seconds. Beat in flour, salt and baking soda on medium speed for 1 minute, scraping bowl occasionally; stir in nuts. Spread in greased and floured 15 x 10 x 1″ jelly roll pan. Bake until light brown, 20 to 25 minutes; cool. Frost and cut into bars.

FROSTING: Mix frosting ingredients together. Stir in 1 to 2 teaspoons additional hot water until smooth and of desired consistency.

Banana Sour Cream Coffee Cake

2 C. flour
1 C. white sugar
1 tsp. baking powder
1 tsp. baking soda
½ tsp. salt
½ tsp. cinnamon
2 eggs

1 tsp. vanilla
½ C. sour cream
1 C. mashed bananas
½ C. butter, softened
½ C. raisins
Powdered sugar, for topping

Combine all ingredients, except powdered sugar; mix until well blended. Pour into a well greased bundt pan. Bake at 350° for 45 minutes. Cool 5 minutes before removing from pan. Sprinkle with powdered sugar and serve warm.

Banana-Rhubarb Pie

2-9" pie crusts
1 lb. (3 C.) rhubarb, sliced
3 medium ripe bananas,
  peeled and sliced (1 C.)
1 C. sugar
¼ C. orange juice

3 T. flour
¼ tsp. salt
¼ tsp. cinnamon
¼ tsp. nutmeg
1 T. butter or margarine

Combine rhubarb, bananas, sugar, orange juice, flour, salt, cinnamon and nutmeg; turn into pastry lined pie plate. Dot with butter. Preheat oven to 450°. Place top crust on filling; cut vents. Bake 15 minutes. Reduce oven temperature to 350° and bake for 30 minutes longer or until pie is brown. Cool completely.

Banana Coffee Cake

1-8 oz. pkg. cream cheese, softened
½ C. butter or margarine, softened
1¼ C. sugar
2 eggs
1 C. mashed ripe bananas
   (about 3 medium)
1 tsp. vanilla extract

2¼ C. all-purpose flour
1½ tsp. baking powder
½ tsp. baking soda
TOPPING:
1 C. chopped pecans
2 T. sugar
1 tsp. ground cinnamon

In a mixing bowl, beat the cream cheese, butter and sugar. Add eggs, one at a time, beating well after each addition. Add bananas and vanilla. Combine flour, baking powder and baking soda; gradually add to the creamed mixture. Combine topping ingredients; add half to batter. Transfer to a greased 13 x 9 x 2″ baking pan. Sprinkle with the remaining topping. Bake at 350° for 25 to 30 minutes or until toothpick inserted near the center comes out clean. Cool on a wire rack.

Banana Cupcakes

2 or 3 ripe bananas
2 tsp. lemon juice
⅔ C. milk
2½ C. flour
1⅔ C. sugar

1¼ tsp. baking powder
1 tsp. baking soda
1 tsp. salt
⅔ C. oil
2 eggs

Mash bananas. Add lemon juice to milk; stir into bananas. Set aside. Preheat oven to 350°. In a large bowl, combine dry ingredients, oil and bananas; mix well. Add eggs and continue beating. Fill cupcake papers two-thirds full and bake for 20 minutes. Dust with powdered sugar after they are removed from the oven.

Banana Yogurt Trifles

2 medium ripe bananas, sliced
⅓ C. orange juice

6 slices angel food cake, cubed
2-8 oz. cartons strawberry-banana
    yogurt

In a bowl, toss the bananas with orange juice. Layer half of the cake cubes in 4 dessert dishes. Top with half the bananas and then half of yogurt. Repeat layers.

Banana Split Pie

3 medium bananas
1 T. lemon juice
1-9″ baked pastry shell, cooled
1 pt. strawberry ice cream

1 C. frozen whipped topping, thawed
Whole maraschino cherries
2 T. finely chopped nuts
Canned chocolate sauce

Thinly slice bananas; sprinkle with lemon juice and arrange on bottom of pastry shell. Stir ice cream to soften; spread on top of bananas. Freeze firm. Spread whipped topping over ice cream layer. Top with maraschino cherries and sprinkle with nuts. Return to freezer. Freeze firm. Before serving, remove pie from freezer and let stand at room temperature for 30 minutes. Serve with chocolate sauce.

Banana Bread Pudding

4 C. cubed day-old bread
¼ C. butter or margarine, melted
3 eggs
2 C. milk
½ C. sugar
2 tsp. vanilla extract
½ tsp. ground cinnamon
½ tsp. ground nutmeg
½ tsp. salt
1 C. sliced firm bananas

SAUCE:
3 T. butter or margarine
2 T. sugar
1 T. cornstarch
¾ C. milk
¼ C. light corn syrup
1 tsp. vanilla extract

(continued on next page)

Place the bread cubes in a greased 2-quart casserole; pour butter over and toss to coat. In a medium bowl, lightly beat eggs. Add milk, sugar, vanilla, cinnamon, nutmeg and salt. Stir in bananas. Pour over bread cubes and stir to coat. Bake, uncovered, at 375° for 40 minutes or until a knife inserted near the center comes out clean. Meanwhile for sauce, melt butter in a small saucepan. Combine sugar and cornstarch; add to butter. Stir in milk and corn syrup. Cook and stir over medium heat until mixture comes to a full boil. Boil for 1 minute. Remove from heat. Stir in vanilla. Serve warm sauce over warm pudding.

Strawberry Banana Split Cake

2 C. graham cracker crumbs
  (about 32 squares)

FILLING:
½ C. butter or margarine, softened
2 C. confectioners' sugar
1 T. milk
1 tsp. vanilla extract

TOPPING:
2 C. whipping cream
¼ C. confectioners' sugar

½ C. butter or margarine, melted
¼ C. sugar

3 large firm bananas, cut into
  ¼″ slices
2-8 oz. cans crushed pineapple,
  drained
2 qts. fresh strawberries, sliced

1½ C. chopped walnuts

(continued on next page)

Combine the crumbs, butter and sugar; press into an ungreased 13 x 9 x 2″ dish. Chill for 1 hour. In a mixing bowl, cream butter, confectioners' sugar, milk and vanilla. Spread over crust; chill for 30 minutes. Layer with bananas, pineapple and strawberries. In a small mixing bowl, beat cream until soft peaks form. Add confectioners' sugar; beat until stiff peaks form. Spread over fruit. Sprinkle with nuts. Chill until serving.

Banana Butterfinger Pudding

1 C. cold milk
1-3.4 oz. pkg. instant banana
  pudding mix
3-2.1 oz. Butterfinger candy bars, crushed

1-8 oz. carton whipped topping,
  thawed
3 medium, firm bananas, sliced

In a mixing bowl, combine milk and pudding; mix until thickened and smooth. Set aside ⅓ cup crushed candy bars for topping. Fold whipped topping, bananas and remaining candy bars into pudding. Spoon into serving dishes; refrigerate until ready to serve. Sprinkle with reserved candy bars.

Banana Spice Cookies

½ C. shortening
1 C. packed brown sugar
2 eggs
1 C. mashed ripe bananas
2 C. all-purpose flour
2 tsp. baking powder

½ tsp. ground cinnamon
¼ tsp. baking soda
¼ tsp. ground cloves
¼ tsp. salt
½ C. chopped walnuts
½ C. raisins

In a mixing bowl, cream shortening and brown sugar. Add eggs and bananas; mix well. Combine dry ingredients; add to creamed mixture and mix well. Stir in nuts and raisins. Chill (dough will be very soft). Drop by rounded teaspoonfuls onto greased baking sheet. Bake at 350° for 8 to 10 minutes or until lightly browned.

Sugar-Free Date Coffee Cake

⅓ C. mashed banana
½ C. margarine
3 eggs
1 tsp. vanilla
1¼ C. water

3 C. flour
1 tsp. baking soda
2 tsp. baking powder
1½ C. chopped dates

Beat together mashed banana and margarine until creamy. Add eggs, vanilla and water; beat. Add dry ingredients and beat. Stir in dates. Spoon batter into 9 x 12″ greased baking dish. Spread batter evenly. Sprinkle on the topping.

TOPPING:
⅓ C. chopped dates
⅓ C. chopped nuts

⅓ C. flaked coconut

Combine topping ingredients and sprinkle over batter. Bake at 350° for 20 to 25 minutes or until done.

Banana Oatmeal Cookies

1⅓ C. flour
¾ C. sugar
½ C. butter
3 T. milk
1 egg, beaten

½ C. mashed banana
½ tsp. baking soda
½ tsp. cinnamon
2 C. oatmeal
1 tsp. vanilla

Cream sugar and butter. Add egg, milk, vanilla and mashed bananas. Sift together flour, baking soda and cinnamon. Add to mixture. Stir in oatmeal. Drop by spoonfuls onto a greased cookie sheet. Bake at 350° for 10 minutes.

Banana Cream Pie

1 C. cold milk
1-3.4 oz. pkg. instant vanilla
   pudding mix
½ tsp. vanilla extract

1-12 oz. carton frozen whipped
   topping, thawed, divided
1-9″ graham cracker crust
2 medium, firm bananas, sliced

In a mixing bowl, beat the milk and pudding mix on low speed for 2 minutes. Beat in vanilla. Fold in 3 cups whipped topping. Pour 1⅓ cups of pudding mixture into pie crust. Layer with banana slices and remaining pudding mixture. Top with remaining whipped topping. Garnish with additional banana slices if desired. Refrigerate until serving.

Chocolate Banana Berry Trifle

1-20 oz. pkg. brownie mix
2 C. sliced strawberries
2 bananas, sliced

4 pkgs. chocolate-covered English
   toffee bars, chopped
2-8 oz. tubs whipped topping, thawed

Prepare and bake brownie mix as package directs. Cool completely in pan on wire rack. Cut into ½˝ squares. Layer half of the brownies, strawberries, bananas, chopped candy bars and whipped topping in a 4-quart serving bowl. Repeat layers. Refrigerate at least 1 hour or until ready to serve. Garnish with additional chopped candy bars, if desired.

Banana Mallow Pie

2 C. vanilla wafer crumbs
½ C. butter, melted
1-3⅛ oz. pkg. instant
  vanilla pudding

1¾ C. milk
1½ C. miniature marshmallows
1 C. whipped topping
2 bananas, sliced

Combine vanilla wafer crumbs and butter. Press into 9″ pie plate. Bake at 375° for 8 minutes. Prepare the pudding; chill. Fold in miniature marshmallows and whipped topping. Slice bananas into crust. Pour filling over bananas. Chill several hours or overnight.

Banana Cake

CAKE:
Yellow cake mix
2 eggs
½ C. oil
1 tsp. soda
2 ripe bananas, mashed

FROSTING:
1 C. cold milk
1 pkg. instant vanilla pudding
¼ C. powdered sugar
1-8 oz. carton whipped topping

CAKE: Mix cake ingredients together and bake at 350°.

FROSTING: Mix first three frosting ingredients until thick, then fold in one 8-ounce carton whipped topping.

Banana Jumbos

1 C. butter or margarine
1 C. sugar
2 eggs
1 C. mashed ripe bananas
  (2 to 3 bananas)
½ C. buttermilk

1 tsp. vanilla
3 C. flour
1½ tsp. soda
½ tsp. salt
1 C. chopped nuts

Mix butter, sugar and eggs thoroughly. Stir in bananas, buttermilk and vanilla. Combine flour, soda and salt; stir into banana mixture. Blend in nuts. Chill for 1 hour. Heat oven to 375°. Drop rounded tablespoonfuls of dough, 2″ apart, onto lightly greased baking sheet. Bake about 10 minutes or until delicately browned. If desired, frost with a thin confectioners' sugar icing.

Cake In A Punch Bowl

1 yellow cake mix, baked and cubed
2 large boxes vanilla instant pudding
5 C. milk
1-15¼ oz. can crushed pineapple,
   undrained

1 qt. strawberries, sliced
3 bananas, sliced
1-16 oz. carton whipped topping
Nuts for top

Bake cake as directed. Cool and cut into cubes. Put in the bottom of a punch bowl.
Mix pudding mix with milk. Pour over cake. Layer the rest of the ingredients and
refrigerate.

Just Like Heaven Cake

1 box yellow cake mix
1 large can crushed pineapple
3 bananas
1 box instant vanilla pudding

1-9 oz. whipped topping
Coconut
Mixed nuts

Mix cake according to directions and bake in 9 x 13″ pan. While cake is still warm, pour over crushed pineapple (well drained), then top with bananas (sliced). Mix pudding and pour over cake. Frost with whipped topping. Top with coconut and mixed nuts (chopped). Keep refrigerated.

Banana and Blueberry Pie

1-1.3 oz. env. whipped topping mix
1-8 oz. pkg. cream cheese, softened
½ C. sugar

3 bananas
2-9″ baked pie shells
1-21 oz. can blueberry pie filling

Prepare whipped topping mix according to package directions. Combine whipped topping, cream cheese and sugar. Beat until creamy. Slice bananas into pie shells. Top with whipped topping mixture. Spread pie filling over top. Chill.

Banana Angel Food Dessert

Angel food cake, broken up
2 pkgs. banana pudding
3½ C. milk

3 bananas
8 oz. whipped topping
⅔ C. almonds

Put angel food pieces in a 9 x 13″ pan. Mix pudding and milk; cook as directed. Cool and spread over cake. Slice bananas on top. Cover with whipped topping and almonds; refrigerate.

Hummingbird Cake

3 C. flour
2 C. sugar
1 tsp. salt
1 tsp. soda
1 tsp. cinnamon
1½ tsp. vanilla

1½ C. oil
3 eggs, beaten
1½ C. crushed pineapple
1½ C. mashed bananas
1 C. chopped nuts

With a large spoon, mix eggs and oil and stir into dry ingredients. Add vanilla, pineapple, bananas and nuts. Bake in three layer cake pans for 30 minutes at 350°. Cool on wire rack and ice.

ICING:
1-8 oz. pkg. cream cheese
½ stick margarine

1 lb. box confectioners' sugar
Small amount milk

Have all ingredients at room temperature. Cream margarine and cheese. Add sugar, small amount at a time. Add milk if needed.

Layered Pudding Dessert

1 C. crushed vanilla wafers, divided
1-3 oz. pkg. cook and serve vanilla
  pudding

2 medium ripe bananas, divided
1-3 oz. strawberry gelatin
1 C. whipped topping

Spread half of the crushed wafers in the bottom of a greased 8″ square pan. Prepare pudding mix according to package. Spoon hot pudding over crumbs. Slice 1 banana; place over pudding. Top with remaining crumbs. Chill for 1 hour. Meanwhile prepare gelatin according to package. Chill for 30 minutes or until partially set. Pour over crumbs. Slice remaining banana and place over gelatin. Spread whipped topping over all. Chill 2 hours.

Creamy Gelatin Dessert

1-6 oz. pkg. lemon gelatin
2 C. boiling water
2 C. miniature marshmallows
4 large ripe bananas, cut into
 ¼" slices
1-20 oz. can crushed pineapple

2 C. cold water
½ C. sugar
2 T. all-purpose flour
2 T. butter or margarine
1 C. whipping cream
½ C. chopped walnuts

In a bowl, dissolve gelatin in boiling water. Stir in marshmallows until melted. Stir in bananas. Drain pineapple, reserving juice. Add pineapple and cold water to gelatin mixture; mix well. Pour into a 13 x 9 x 2" pan. Chill until set. In a small saucepan, combine the sugar and flour. Gradually stir in reserved pineapple juice. Add butter. Bring to boil; cook and stir for 2 minutes. Remove from heat; cool to room temperature, about 35 to 40 minutes. Whip the cream; fold in pineapple juice mixture. Spread over gelatin. Sprinkle with nuts. Chill for 1 to 2 hours.

Banana Upside-Down Cake

½ C. packed brown sugar
2 T. lemon juice
1 T. butter or margarine

CAKE:
1½ C. all-purpose flour
½ C. sugar
1 tsp. baking soda
1 tsp. baking powder
¼ tsp. salt

½ C. pecan halves
2 medium-firm bananas

¼ C. cold butter or margarine
1 C. plain yogurt
2 eggs, beaten
2 tsp. grated lemon peel
1 tsp. vanilla

(continued on next page)

In a small saucepan, combine brown sugar, 1 tablespoon lemon juice and butter; bring to a boil. Reduce heat to medium; cook without stirring until sugar is dissolved. Pour into a greased 9″ springform pan. Arrange pecans on top with flat side up. Pour remaining lemon juice into a small bowl. Add bananas and stir carefully; drain. Arrange bananas in a circular pattern over pecans; set aside. In a large bowl, combine flour, sugar, baking soda, baking powder and salt. Cut in butter until mixture resembles coarse crumbs. Combine yogurt, eggs, lemon peel and vanilla; stir into the dry ingredients just until moistened. Spoon over bananas. Bake at 375° for 35 to 40 minutes or until a toothpick inserted near center comes out clean. Cool for 10 minutes. Run knife around edge of pan; invert cake onto a serving plate. Serve with whipped cream.

Banana Split Dessert

18 squares graham crackers
3 bananas, sliced
½ gal. carton strawberry ice cream
1 C. chopped walnuts
1 C. chocolate chips

½ C. butter
2 C. powdered sugar
1½ C. evaporated milk
1 tsp. vanilla
2 C. whipped topping

Arrange graham crackers in bottom of 9 x 13″ pan. Layer bananas, ½″ thick slices of ice cream and walnuts over graham crackers. Freeze until firm. Melt chocolate chips and butter in saucepan. Add powdered sugar, evaporated milk and vanilla. Cook over medium heat until thickened, stirring constantly. Cool. Pour over ice cream. Freeze until firm. Top with whipped topping. Freeze until firm. Remove from freezer 10 minutes before serving. Garnish with maraschino cherries if desired.

Bananas Foster

½ C. butter
1 C. brown sugar
8 ripe bananas

Cinnamon to taste
6 oz. rum or rum extract

Melt butter in frying pan over medium-low heat. Stir in brown sugar. Slice bananas thinly lengthwise. Add to brown sugar mixture. Cook until tender. Sprinkle with cinnamon. Add rum. Cook until bubbly. Remove from heat. Ignite sauce; allow flames to die down. Serve immediately.

Frosted Banana Bars

½ C. butter, softened
2 C. sugar
3 eggs
1 to 1½ C. mashed ripe bananas
  (about 3)

1 tsp. vanilla
2 C. flour
1 tsp. baking soda
Pinch of salt

FROSTING:
½ C. butter, softened
1-8 oz. pkg. cream cheese, softened

4 C. powdered sugar
2 tsp. vanilla

In a mixing bowl, cream butter and sugar. Beat in eggs, bananas and vanilla. Combine the flour, baking soda and salt; add to creamed mixture and mix well. Pour into a greased 10 x 15″ baking pan. Bake at 350° for 25 minutes or until bars test done; cool.

FROSTING: Cream butter and cream cheese in a mixing bowl. Gradually add powdered sugar and vanilla; beat well. Spread over bars.

Banana Boats

8 firm bananas
40 miniature marshmallows

1 C. miniature chocolate chips

Peel back a long strip of banana peel on the inside curve of each banana, leaving bottom end of strip attached. Scoop out some of the banana. Fill scooped-out space with 5 miniature marshmallows and ⅛ cup miniature chocolate chips. Replace banana peel. Wrap tightly in foil. Bake at 350° for 15 to 20 minutes or until heated through.

Chocolate-Bottom Banana Bars

½ C. butter
1 C. sugar
1 egg
1 tsp. vanilla
1 to 1½ C. mashed ripe bananas
   (about 3)

1½ C. flour
1 tsp. baking powder
1 tsp. baking soda
½ tsp. salt
¼ C. cocoa

In a mixing bowl, cream butter and sugar. Add egg and vanilla; beat until thoroughly combined. Blend in the bananas. Combine flour, baking powder, baking soda and salt; add to creamed mixture and mix well. Divide batter in half. Add cocoa to half; spread into a greased 9 x 13″ baking pan. Spoon remaining batter on top and swirl with a knife. Bake at 350° for 25 minutes or until the bars test done. Cool.

Banana S'mores

¾ C. graham cracker crumbs
½ C. Bisquick baking mix
2 T. sugar
¼ C. butter, melted
2 or 3 medium bananas

3 T. lemon juice
1⅓ C. milk
1-3½ oz. pkg. instant vanilla pudding
¾ C. miniature marshmallows
16 chocolate stars

Mix cracker crumbs, baking mix and sugar; stir in butter until moistened. Press in bottom of square microwavable dish, 8 x 8 x 2″. Microwave, uncovered, on high, rotating dish ½ turn every minute, until crust bubbles up slightly and then begins to flatten, 1½ to 3 minutes. Cool 10 minutes on wire rack. Slice bananas; dip into lemon juice and arrange on crust. Beat milk and pudding mix until smooth. Stir in marshmallows. Spread pudding mixture over banana slices; press chocolate stars onto pudding mixture. Refrigerate no longer than 1 hour if desired.

Banana Sorbet in Orange Shells

1⅓ C. sugar
1½ C. water
6 navel oranges

4 large ripe bananas, peeled
and chilled
¼ C. freshly squeezed lemon juice

In a small saucepan over medium heat, cook sugar and water, stirring constantly, just until mixture boils. Remove from heat and cool slightly; then chill in refrigerator at least 1 hour or until cold. Halve oranges and squeeze each half gently to make approximately 2 cups of juice. With a spoon, carefully scrape pulp from each orange half; discard pulp. Cover shells with plastic wrap and refrigerate until serving time. In a food processor or blender, purée bananas until smooth. Add orange juice, lemon juice and chilled sugar syrup; process until smooth. Pour into a large metal pan or bowl; freeze until solid. Remove from freezer; process until creamy; refreeze until firm. Scoop out a ½ cup of sorbet into each orange-shell half.

Index

Appetizers & Beverages

Salads & Veggies

Main Dishes

Desserts